W0016884

The Tongues of Men and of Angels

The Tongues
of Men and of
Angels

Robert A. Fink

Texas Tech University Press

Copyright 1995 Texas Tech University Press

All rights reserved. No portion of this book may be reproduced in any form or by any means, including electronic storage and retrieval systems, except by explicit, prior written permission of the publisher except for brief passages excerpted for review and critical purposes.

This book was set in Goudy Old Style and printed on acid-free paper that meets the guidelines for permanence and durability of the Committee on Production Guidelines for Book Longevity of the Council on Library Resources.

Printed in the United States of America

Jacket design Ted Genoways

Library of Congress Cataloging-in-Publication Data

Fink, Robert Adon.
    The tongues of men and of angels / Robert A. Fink.
        p. cm.
    ISBN 0-89672-341-0 (alk. paper)
    I. Title.
    PS3556.I4756T65   1995
811'.54—dc20   94-46581
                                                              CIP

95 96 97 98 99 00 01 02 03 / 9 8 7 6 5 4 3 2 1

Texas Tech University Press
P. O. Box 41037
Lubbock, Texas 79409-1037 USA
1-800-832-4042

ACKNOWLEDGMENTS

These poems, several in earlier versions, first appeared in the following publications, to whom grateful acknowledgment is made:

Borderlands: Texas Poetry Review: "Breakdown"
English Journal: "Procreation"
Graham House Review: "After Athens, Paul Refuses to Use the Devices of Greek Philosophy"; "Laying On Of Hands"; "Nearing the End of His Journey, Paul Considers What Comfort He Has Brought His Friends"
Harvard Magazine: "The Hot Corner"
Looking For Your Name (New York: Orchard Books): "To My Sons on Father's Day"; "Why Is It"
New Texas 91: "What It Takes"
New Texas 92: "Welcome Home, Stranger"
Rocky Mountain Review: "1951, His Father Squeezed His Arm"
Southern Poetry Review: "Last Words"

I am especially grateful to Walt McDonald for his encouragement and his insightful editing. And to Daryl Jones for his close reading of the first draft. I am also grateful to Larry Brunner, Scott Cairns, Judith Keeling, George Knight, Bruce Smith, Craig Turner, Delores Washburn, and Chris Willerton for their support and advice.

For Trina

Contents

I

Why Is It   3

1951, His Father Squeezed His Arm   4

Summer of '67   5

For This Cause   6

Following a Sharp Disagreement, Barnabas Breaks From
Paul, Sails With Mark to Cyprus   7

And Who Shall Separate Us?   8

After Athens, Paul Refuses to Use the Devices
of Greek Philosophy   9

Rotation   10

Woodbridge, Virginia, 1971:
The Unfurnished Apartment Overrun, He Calls
a Napalm Strike Upon His Position   11

II

Let Each Man Abide   15

First House   16

Paul Shares His Secret   17

What It Takes   18

In Training   20

The Assistant Professor Considers His Options   21

How He Came to Write Poetry   22

III

Speaking in Tongues: The Calling   25

Courtly Love   26

At Eighteen   27

Last Words   28

Hitting Fungoes After the Funeral   29

Saul Tries to Explain How Hard It Was for the Apostles
to Believe His Conversion   30

The Beach Boys Claimed an Angel Stirred the Waters   31

IV

Marathon   35

Wax Not After the Lusts of Deceit   36

The Ex-Grunt Writes His Last Letter to His Former
Professor   37

A Common Dream   39

Paul Performs a Miracle   40

Homecoming   41

The Hot Corner   43

The Vietnam Vet Looks for His Sons at Summer
Basketball Camp   44

Nearing the End of His Journey, Paul Considers What
Comfort He Has Brought His Friends   45

Procreation   46

V

Touch   49

The Poet Already Missing His Sons   50

Breakdown   52

Welcome Home, Stranger   53

Paul Completes the Path to Sainthood   55

St. Francis of Abilene   57

The Writer-In-Residence Interrupts
My Scheduled Run   58

Just Off Beulah Street   59

Laying On of Hands   61

To My Sons On Father's Day   62

Notes   63

If I come to you speaking with tongues, . . .
how shall it be known what is spoken?

First Corinthians 14: 6,9

I

Who shall separate us
   from the love of Christ?
Shall tribulation, or anguish,
   or persecution, or famine,
or nakedness,
   or peril, or sword?

Romans 8: 35-36a

Why Is It

at the half-price book table in the Mall,
we always find picture histories of war
nobody buys but can't put down—
like when I was a kid in the corner drug
reading comic books flopped on the bottom shelf
of the magazine stand, my father sitting at the counter
buying a Cherry Coke for some high school graduate
home on leave, first time, who just dropped by
the Rexall to parade his uniform?

You know what I mean
and why we can't believe this book—
too many piles of bodies, too many summary hangings
and bullets to the base of the brain
to trust the photographers.

Like the full-page spread
of the lovely Russian girl swinging from a rope
delicate as a necklace of pearls, her head
cocked to one side as if trying to catch
the flattering whisper passed across the aisle in school,
her boyfriend winking he'll meet her later in the grove—
certainly not to shoot at Germans, outside Minsk,
    October, 1941;
certainly not to find themselves hanged together in a barn
by curious soldiers who seem to want to touch
the girl's taut breast, smooth back her tousled hair,
even rub a finger along her full, protruding lower lip.

1951, His Father Squeezed His Arm,

told the joke stark as bed sheets
flapping on a backyard line,
mother clothespinning blouses, slips, his short pants
side by side—a message to the neighbors
like the string of flags on cruisers
he cut out from backs of cereal boxes,
pasted together on the dotted lines,
repeating out loud *Korea.* He was Ali Baba,
the word would sail his daddy home

in a red silk jacket, a tiger snarling on the back.
His father limped into the house, pulled off his boots
and rolled the socks down where his toes had been.
This little piggy went to town
over and over—the punch line
suffered too many times to smile,
to believe in magic: words
that roll back stone,
that heal the lame, the blind.

Summer of '67

Like sparrows flocking to telephone lines,
we'd take our place each morning
at the ten o'clock break, squat on the curb,
Lankersham Boulevard, North Hollywood, California:
college students drawn from the beach
to hammer out interview booths for marketing research—
plywood pulpits, '60s evangelists.

Oh we were rich, whistling at miniskirts
stopping traffic. We shouted movie contracts
if only they'd walk our way
past the storefront window taped with butcher paper
teasing the neighborhood with our intentions,
as if the quickdraw artist tooling holsters for TV cowboys
cared about the banging going on next door,
as if Sal who ran the hot dog stand on the corner
really believed we were C.I.A.
High noon, a black limo idled for an Orange Julius.
We took Sal's chili dogs over for a peep inside
the tinted windows, reported back,
"Bond, James Bond." 007. License to kill.

We were flying high as cherries on Sal's cheesecake,
as Universal Studios rising in the east.
So we sang along, cruising Wonderland,
MacArthur Park melting in the dark
like napalm on the evening news
tumbling after Alice down the rabbit hole
to swallow pills—one to explode you
through the jungle's triple canopy,
one to shrink you back to dust,
the rabbit white and still
beside you, his open mouth a curse.

For This Cause

She knocked on his door past midnight
to ask was it true
he'd enlisted in the Marines.
He thought she meant the uniform:
its priestly collar, the red stripe of courage
running down each leg,
the ceremonial sword—double edged
to keep young officers gentlemen.
What she must have meant
was jungle rot, malaria,
shit-tipped punji sticks.
He answered *yes* and, courteously,
did not invite her in.

Following a Sharp Disagreement, Barnabas
Breaks From Paul, Sails With Mark to Cyprus

After the Damascus road, no sudden loss
is more than I can bear, but I regret
sharp words over giving Mark a second chance.
They cost me Barnabas.
His leaving grieves me like a thorn.

How hard it is to give up being Saul.
My temper shakes me like a child
possessed by demons, causing him to fall
sometimes in fire, sometimes in water.
I take small consolation remembering
God made me what I am.

And Who Shall Separate Us?

He had been in Nam so long
he no longer spoke
except in numbers
from the mimeographed sheet
issued first day in country.

    #37: "Not another —— second lieutenant!"
    #117: "Where's my —— jeep?"
    #269: "Obviously you have me confused
             with someone who gives a ——."

He stopped hearing profanity
the second week, stopped wasting breath
when the rocket hit the sky pilot's hut, no one left
to pray for souls bartered in Bangkok–
overnight flights to bar girls
almost younger than sisters back home
giggling on the telephone over who likes whom,
never dreaming, in their pink canopy beds,
anything worth confessing.

After Athens, Paul Refuses to Use the Devices
of Greek Philosophy

At Thessalonica, even the gang of market place toughs
honored, in their ignorance, our work.
They stirred a crowd, set off
an uproar throughout the city:
"They who have turned the world upside down are here!"
I couldn't ask for a better introduction.

But Athens!
It is easier for a rich man
to pass stiff-necked through the needle's eye
than for an intellectual.
These Epicureans, these Stoics
worship their graven arts, the brass tinkle
of their syllogisms. They nudge
each other in the ribs and giggle.
They led me to the Areopagus
thinking to prod me like a dancing bear
for their amusement, their only diversion
to tell, to hear, some new idea.
I had to shout above the din of voices
clamoring for the floor—waves crashing on rocks.

They smiled behind their hands
when I proclaimed the stone rolled back,
Christ risen from the tomb.
Someone shouted, "Maybe another time
would be best to hear of this."
Their laughter dogged me past the city limits.
I shook their dusty logic off my feet.

Rotation

It was the day
he never thought would come,
the day he survived
to almost talk about
back home, in the states,
his morning cup of coffee cooling
in the ceramic mug—
Have A Good Day
stenciled beneath a smiling sun,
its eyes the neat holes
of a sniper's bullet.
At the kitchen table!
His wife as close to naked
as neighbors allowed,
folding his hands in hers
as if they both could pray,
as if every husband in the states
couldn't lift his morning coffee
without spilling half, weeping
at the heft of this mug.
No more styrofoam
he could snap with his teeth
and chew when he mustn't talk.
Imagine this day, how difficult
not to X it off on the calendar
as if he hadn't made it
home to the woman
any man would kill to get back to.

Woodbridge, Virginia, 1971: The Unfurnished
Apartment Overrun, He Calls a Napalm Strike
Upon His Position

Those upon the ground believed
a star had fallen, a dollop of sun—
molten tsunami crashing upon their huts.
He prayed this scene would fall from his eyes
like scales of the dragon
hunched along the China Sea, its spine
a coast of concertina wire and human waste.

Why him? No Saul. No chosen vessel.
So inconspicuous no one would entrust
garments at his feet or care if he consented
to the nightmare slamming him,
this February weekend, prone
on the floor, clutching a pillow
like Jacob's stone, like the angel—
his only hope of a blessing.

He snatched a breath
and buried his face in the pillow,
counting to 60 for the wrath of God to pass
melting a layer of flesh from his back.
To scream meant he would swallow fire,
die a hero remembering only
a great light, voices
crying in the wilderness.

Then he heard a knock upon the door
and understood he would live,
how many things he would be asked to suffer.

II

Let each man abide in that calling
wherein he was called.

First Corinthians 7:20

Let Each Man Abide

You never dreamed you'd end up
on the road from Abilene to Lubbock,
new phase of the moon, no coyote
silhouetted on the backdrop mesa,
not even a vagrant star
to confirm the desert
outside your window.

No settler wandered here on purpose
unless, three days gone on peyote,
he'd risen from his body
to walk dry-shod the bottom of the sea,
pass through the fire by night
to God's distant promise: Land!
A vision burned in stone.

Not yours!
A woman brought you here
where standing back to back
you could recognize, a long way off,
trouble coming and arm yourself,
Defender Of The Hearth,
or slam the kitchen door,
burn off in the pickup,

nothing out there
interfering with the ball game
coming in from someplace green
contained by fences, extra innings
where, called from the bench,
you rise, shoulder your bat,
square up against a grinning reliever.

First House

No board that did not give,
no sphere that would not roll
when set down carefully,
any point upon the floor—
a cosmos askew,
a twelve-foot-ceiling house
where anything might happen:

the woman sitting up in bed
to call his name, faint signal
homing in the outer reaches
of his nightly orbit
connecting dots of light,
the fragile constellation
of full-length windows
a sparrow could shatter.

He had to touch each pane,
check off the thirty ways
to see himself darkly
before he'd come full circle
back to the woman
pulling him in.

Paul Shares His Secret

God's home is in our hands
casting a net, guiding
a needle through canvas.

I laid my hands upon the twelve at Ephesus:
God sparked from my fingers.
Believers touch me with their handkerchiefs
and carry Jehovah to bedridden friends,
children possessed by spirits.

God shaped Adam from the soil of Eden.
Satan taught the other function of the hand
discovered by the seven sons of Sceva.
They wrung their hands and cried,
"We adjure you by the Jesus invoked by Paul."
The demon was not fooled: "Jesus I recognize,
and Paul I know, but who are you?" It drove them
stripped and bleeding into the street.

Consider the boy Eutychus
perched on the windowsill, attending to my sermon
until the flesh was overcome by sleep.
He fell three stories in the dream
unbelievers claim one cannot wake from.
I held him in my arms and felt again God's joy,
the Creator's fingers kneading clay.
They took the boy away alive. I returned upstairs
and, with these hands, broke bread.

What It Takes

He eased his hand from hers
and kissed her hair, walked out
to the reflection pond,
the moon on the water
female, pliable as a fertile egg
dividing.

At his back: hospital walls
black as the castle keep,
a light burning in the only window
that mattered—his wife propped in bed,
staring at the space between her arms.
Her babies waited in a glass womb—
tubes and monitors, a pump
risky as a gypsy's concertina.

He unbuckled his sword,
laid it hilt-first toward the water,
bowed his head, and kneeling,
offered the nape of his neck.
Unacceptable. He lifted up the football game,
his jaw broken in three places,
the head of Christ appearing
in blood on his jersey.
The letter of introduction from the King.
The key pressed into his palm
by the Homecoming Queen.

He had known all along what was needed.
He took off his letter jacket,
the coat of mail, the hair shirt,
then lifted the ribbon over his head—
a silk remembrance blue as the sky

falling, a cluster of thirteen stars
knotted at his throat.
Beneath the cerulean dome,
a golden anchor linked the heavens
to his world, five-pointed
as the star the marshal unpins from his shirt,
blood soaking through a sleeve,
his long-barreled Colt still smoking.

He held the medal one last time,
shut his eyes, and slung it over the water.
He listened for the splash,
then turned to the window, his wife
risen from her bed, laughing,
holding out his newborn sons.

In Training

She plies you with granola:
raw oats, lightly scorched
to discourage horses.
The good germs of wheat—
her favorite chunky plumbers
with their roto-rooter.
Bran, bitter as a dead
grandmother's liver.
Raisins adhesive as rabbit turds.
Shredded coconut—
dried, cross sections of tongue.
All buffeted in a Beatrix Potter bowl
of no-percent milk the texture of mucus.

Toddlers gesture from highchairs,
waving their swill-dripping spoons
like gluttonous minor officials
of the Roman senate, Nero's distant kin,
mouths brimming over
calling for dancing girls:
Let the games begin.
Your wife hums, happy in her route
between the breakfast table and the sink,
a Christian grateful for the lions—
her victory. Yours, the marathon
she shapes you toward, the long haul
from corruptible to a body purged of flesh,
puerile as the dreams of angels.

The toddlers bang their plastic cups
for *meat! meat!* Your wife
skips to their side and spoons it in.
They open wide to show you what you're missing.

The Assistant Professor Considers His Options

You know the stories—
the concupiscence of coeds
needing a higher grade, revealing
in the privacy of your office
an eagerness to do whatever it takes.
"Anything?" you're supposed to ask.
She slides her tongue across her lips,
bends down and whispers, "Yes. . . ."
Your punch line is: "Try studying!"
An old joke she won't care for,
nor you.

How did you get so good?
You probably won't make tenure
and no one believes your marriage will last
but you and the little woman
who, still in her floor-length, flannel nightgown,
toddlers tugging at her thighs,
selects the sharpest
from a drawer of kitchen knives.

How He Came to Write Poetry

He'd bolt awake at 4:00 a.m.,
the dream wrapped round him
like an umbilical cord, a pet boa constrictor
loving him to death. He'd reach out
for his wife, hold on
until his breathing almost matched
her steady pace—the heavy footfalls
of a mother bringing that glass of water
in the night, sealing the closet door
against those childhood sins,
sharp-toothed and noisy.

When he believed he had not fallen
among thieves, had not been cast
into a bog of hogs
huffing their decayed breath
in his face, their dung-nosed piglets
squealing, "Your old man loves his migrant workers
more than you," he'd rise
and walk to the bedsides of his sons,
adjust their covers in case they stirred,
questioning his need to kiss each on the cheek,
whisper, "It was just a dream.
Daddy's here. Go back to sleep."

III

Though I speak with the tongues
   of men and of angels
but have not love,
   I am become as sounding brass
or a clanging cymbal.

First Corinthians 13:1

Speaking in Tongues: The Calling

I saw her rise from the bed
of a 1950s pickup, spread her arms
to take in the potholed street,
snap back her head—the hair
straight and long as the path to God,
black as Elijah's ravens feeding him beak to tongue
the song of thunder across the desert.

I inched closer with the other boys
out for kicks on a Saturday night, believing
we'd come for the bootlegger's daughter
speaking only the language of coins
ringing in the coffer, not this angel
ascending a ladder of words
I didn't know but bowed before,
and in the dust, scratched with my finger
what I suddenly understood
my God! was *joy*, language
no one could honor in this country.

Courtly Love

In his father's Ford by the lake,
the late August moon bright as a mirror
cocked to catch the sun, they held each other
in the drama of teenagers about to part.
She lay her head against his heart
like in the movies
and said if they stayed much longer
she could like him too much
if he knew what she meant.
He kissed her hair
then tilted up her chin, met once more
those lips discreetly parting
and thought she wanted him
to take her home.

Oh, winding back through the woods
on the moonlit road, he was puffed up
sounding off his future
brassy as Rossini's Overture—
all things certain to climax
with him masked, raring high
on a white stallion: Hi-Yo, Silver, Away!

He believed Love saved herself
for the moving of mountains,
the mystery of revelation
on the wedding night—
all dragons slain, all stones
finally labored from the sea.

At Eighteen

Thou shalt not dream
wheels of fire
burning up all roads
from here to there,
all bridges caving in
in flames.

Thou shalt not
enter the house
of your best girl's mom
when she opens the door
to say Alicia's spending the night
with her father, nobody's home,
come in.

Thou shalt not
catch thy father's fist
mid-punch and bend it back
until you hear the crack
like a hinge forced against itself,
screws tearing loose.

Last Words

1.

In all the matinees your father walked you to
those Saturdays before you'd grown to fit the bike
he bought on sale and hid till Christmas,
the dying cowboy always said:
"Tell Nell I was true."
"It's nothing; just another bullet."
"You must go on . . . without me."
He'd place you in line,
hand over the quarter,
a dime for popcorn,
the extra nickel for Charms,
then fold your fingers around the coins.

When the show let out, he'd be waiting
in the sunlight rising from the sidewalk.
You shaded your eyes and stumbled
toward your name, the weight
of his hand on your shoulder.

2.

Had he stayed for those movies,
he'd have known not to choose
"I guess you'll be driving back now."
Who could blame you
for not believing this The End—
words carried home
like a fist in your pocket.

Hitting Fungoes After the Funeral

High noon, you take the bat,
the sack of balls
you rummaged from the attic
to the high school diamond
where your father never missed a game,
recording every error.
The bat, he liked to say,
is thin as fame,
long as a washboard road
shaking, by God, some sense
into your skull like the light
so harsh you believe the voice
Jehovah's bean ball knocking you down
until you cry *My God! My God!* rise
and blindly drive each ball
into his eye and swear five hundred times,
I forgive you! I forgive you!

Saul Tries to Explain How Hard It Was
for the Apostles to Believe His Conversion

Consider Judas.
Surprised at the part he played,
he ran to return the silver,
be born again.
The priests dismissed him with a curse.
Suppose that when he flung the coins,
each piece caught the light,
wings of doves descending.

What if now he had a sin worth pardoning
like Peter when he cursed his Lord,
swearing to the courtyard riffraff
he was no follower of the Nazarene,
that bastard carpenter?
What if he fell with Peter to his knees,
wept such bitter tears they turned to joy?

Imagine Judas, the rope around his neck,
not falling headlong
to burst asunder. Imagine
turning back to the apostles
who would not forget
his hand dipped in the dish of Christ,
his kiss of death at Gethsemane.

The Beach Boys Claimed an Angel Stirred the Waters

And I only am escaped alone in my '64 Ford,
its wire-spoked hubcaps spinning
wheel within wheel across the desert night
at ninety miles an hour. Flesh melts by day
into a pile of salt.

This side of Yuma, blue lights
sprinkling the desert floor,
Janis Joplin screamed on the radio.
I took it for a sign
I would enter a second time my mother's womb,
and I knew when the Santa Monica freeway
narrowed to the tunnel opening on the Pacific,
I should leave the car, cast myself
into the hard cold waves.

Even before the scales fell away,
I believed I could see.
Even before the lesions healed,
I believed I was rising from the water
clean.

IV

I, therefore, so run as not uncertainly.
So fight I as not beating the air.

First Corinthians 9:26

Marathon

Books promised the first ten miles easy
as giving up, the body light as lungs
brimming with rarefied air,
flights of angels singing him to rest.

Six miles into the run, his knees
began to click a faint warning
coming in from down the line:
The trestle's out.
They've dumped a dead cow in the spring.
Butch plans to stick his leg across the aisle.

Soon, he knew, the heavenly host
would fill the desert sky,
wings clapping up pillars of sand
to mark his passing, stooped,
one hand shading the eyes
afraid to notice his father
had forgotten the lamb,
did not pass the time with parables—
how the hall-of-fame fireballer
never looked back, how Methuselah
wrote the book on *slow but sure.*

At the twelve-mile water stop,
a jam box blared ". . . bones, dem bones. . . ."
A woman sucking on a lemon
called out, "Looking good! You're halfway home."
Paper cups littered the path like day-old manna.
He bent down beside the woman,
braced his elbows on his knees.
The angels must have come and gone.

Wax Not After the Lusts of Deceit

Think a moment of Paul, the apostle,
having folded up the easy fit of Saul—
that man of thou-shalt-nots
tangible as Law.
Did he shed his old self
easily as a snake?
Or did he sometimes late at night
when only Jehovah was watching,
slip the suit from the bottom
of his bureau drawer and hold it up
before the mirror?

Maybe more than once
he wore it under his homespun robe
to remember God had called him
to take what Stephen took, but rise
from where the Jews had dragged his body,
reenter their city; called him to strike
the fear of God in hearts
of jailers, magistrates
he demanded escort him from prison.

I'm sure he must have worn it
when he entered Rome,
and when, way back at Pamphylia,
he cast off Mark for being young
and homesick, for dropping out
of the race. That slacker.
That poet.

The Ex-Grunt Writes His Last Letter
to His Former Professor

I'm sick of Vietnam, marginal notes
suggesting I buy the latest thriller
spilling it "like it was," sit through the movie
everyone has seen but me.

You say my poems have no life.
I need to show; don't tell.
Open up. Confess
the "truth" of napalm strikes—
backyard barbecues you want to taste.

I guess you mean
slide the reader down a garbage bag;
kick him, hands tied, from a chopper just for fun;
cut out his privates, jam them between his teeth.

How about I take you headfirst
down this tunnel tight as a cat hole?
Mail me the metaphor for an ice pick through the eye.
May I send you twenty ways to slit a throat?
We'll start with tin-can lids.

Pretend I haven't had a bath since Thursday
and my platoon is straggling toward a friendly village
when Hang Ten drops crotch first

into a pit of punji sticks tipped with shit.
Describe the shape a mouth takes before it screams.

Now imagine you live in that village
and I learn you dug the pit.
Look at me!
I've got a razor blade.
I've got your wife.

A Common Dream

Deep in the closet, his father's
wool overcoat hanging before him
like the back of God, he dreamed
his parents had opened their door
to a silk-lined basket, the handmade paper note
tied with purple ribbon. The penmanship
feminine, a flourish of strokes—
vines entwining a tree.
They looked both ways and took him in.

That was thirty years ago.
His father had sent him to the closet
to learn a lesson. A carpenter forgets,
shavings piling up beneath his plane,
that the boy sweating sonnets in the corner
was not born to the doggerel of saw and hammer,
the conjugal rhythms of coarse sandpaper
wearing down oak against the grain.

Paul Performs a Miracle

John Mark laid his hand to the plow
but quit the field at Pamphylia.
He was young and missed his bed,
a street with neighbors
condoning his moods, his latest poem.

Had he been lame from birth
he would have listened like the man at Lystra
when I told him: *Get to your feet!*
The anger in my words was not for him.
It surprised me more than he,
falling at my feet, believing me *Zeus*;
Barnabas, *Hermes*, my messenger.
I confess I wished Mark there to hear the people cry
"The gods have come to us in human form"—
my greatest temptation.

But no mortal who has stared into the sun
can ever see himself more than a mote
in the corner of God's eye.
I fell beside the man and tore my clothes,
exposed my flesh to the stones men always cast
to prove their god.

They dragged me off for dead.
How I wished Mark there when I walked back into town,
proclaimed the risen Lord.

Homecoming

You've been lost before,
never on a road you thought you knew—
the short cut from New Hope to View,
just enough fuel to get you
past the scythes, the S's—*Slow, or Die!*—
the Y's divining secrets.

Farm land spills across the rear view
mirror. You *have* been here before...wheat
to the right of you, wheat
to the left, floorboarding
your old man's Ford down a black-top road
to Quitman, a girl fast as Highway 80. . . .

No. You're boxed, the needle on the gas gauge
redundant as a compass. Then you spy the angel
growing like a speck on the horizon
empty as promise in West Texas. You begin to see
the wings are folded in a V
for *vapid. Vamoose* if you're lucky.

You're not. All along
you knew it was a tractor, the wings
harrow discs honed mirror sharp.
You hunch your neck passing beneath the blades,
wave to the farmer. Maybe he'll lift the hand
cocked above the lever.

Out here they bury evidence,
vehicles plowed under against erosion.
Now you spot the sign:

Nillon 2 Miles where you'll hit *empty*
in a town you know will have a post office,
boarded up since '68, a General Store

with bubble-headed gas pumps—
spacemen who touched down
in a place what don't cotton to strangers.
You're right about the P.O., but the store
sports gas-club pumps, and you ain't a member.
So welcome back where you started

like those boys racing up on balloon-tire bicycles.
You anticipate their easy spirals around the pickup,
their summer drawls slower than the decades
it takes to be a man, the one who'll never get away
reciting the story of his life; the other sizing you up,
deciding if he's big enough to commandeer your truck.

The Hot Corner

This is no place for insouciance
or the casual grace
of the man in center
tossing blades of grass
to chart the drift
of currents he calls friends,
knowing their moods
and how to circumvent them.

The third baseman
has a wife and kids,
always a baby needing shoes,
and he's in a crapshoot
with the dice loaded
against him—the one-hopper
to his groin,
the screaming liner at his skull,
the shot pulled down the line
to clip the bag with him extended
as far as heroically possible
and it ain't enough.

The Vietnam Vet Looks for His Sons
at Summer Basketball Camp

Basketballs drum the floor.
A hundred hearts race up and down the court.
Intent as salmon leaping up the falls,
these middle schoolers drive for backboards,
spin lay ups through the hoops.

Young men on the evening news
slam chunks of metal down a pipe
they aim toward towns
where other boys draw circles in the dirt,
spill out their bags of marbles.

Nearing the End of His Journey, Paul Considers What Comfort He Has Brought His Friends

All my roads lead to Rome.
My friends are blind as Peter swearing
he would save Christ from the cross.
The elders prayed and wept for me at Ephesus.
At Caesarea, the prophet Agabus
thought to break my heart with pantomime—
how at Jerusalem I would be bound hand and foot.
My friends love me as much as I fear God.
I held their hands, assuring them
Jerusalem was not Rome, God works
through nephews, my sister's child—
such a good boy—always listening at doors
to grown-ups' conversations, training his ears
for the whispers of forty, portly Jews
vowing not to drink or eat
till they'd murdered his favorite uncle.
Roman governors and kings
are easy to circumvent. They fear the Law,
defer, except for the lash,
all judgments to higher administrators.
So all roads lead to Caesar
who prides himself a poet, plucking his lyre.
A gong, booming. A clanging cymbal.

Procreation

God must have thought he'd love a crowd.
I'm certain he had in mind a game
with bat and ball, the cool fit
of leather to the hand.
The earth, after all, is round
and rotates like a screwball
breaking in and down.

This may explain why
two who gather on a field
multiply to four, to six.
But next time a father happens up
with his preschooler and a toddler
and asks to take a turn at bat for fun,
my friend who pitched eight years for Philly
serving them up, I'll tell him *No.*
I'm too old to believe
that from deep in the hole
I can cover third a second time
to backhand his shot pulled down the line
homing in on daughters
he promised to mind.

I'm forty-four, no longer God
to teenage sons who field for themselves
and wouldn't be caught on this playground
with their old man and his pals
who thought they were creating
nothing of consequence—
random, casual acts of grace.

V

For by grace have you been saved
   through faith, and that not of yourselves;
it is the gift of God; not of works,
   lest any man should boast.

Ephesians 2: 8-9

Touch

We must be born believing
God patted our bottoms,
sent us in the game
with the winning play, a timing route—
juke & go, sure touchdown,
one step on Defender of Darkness,
the pass predestined for our fingers.

We believe in spite of doctors
smacking our butts until we screamed,
indignant, demanding our mother's nipple,
her breast tapered like the football
we receive, good hands, on fingertips—
cupped supplicants at the shrine of Mother
hugging, kissing us, making it all better.

The Poet Already Missing His Sons

Knowing how teenagers swell
like sponges in sea wash,
tumble out with tides
toward lands too real for fathers,
he chose with care the trappings
of his room, the poet shaping the house
of *touch, taste, smell.*
He dared not trust his eyes—
such five-year-olds peeping over
the banister Christmas morning.

He fashioned four white walls—
screens for the magic lantern show:
Crayon-printed rhymes his mother pasted
in the spiral notebook. The thighs
of Sunday women posing on the beach.
The girl he followed first grade to graduation
behind the waterfall—that first room
imagination fit.

He scoured the derelict district
for his writing table, rescued
like a pup from the pound
to grow old and grateful at his feet—
good servant, never out past midnight
casting off the edge of oceans, never
battened down behind a Keep Out sign
humming chanteys to himself.
He hoped he'd find beneath the palimpsest of paint—
oak, the planking of Magellan's ship.

Each dawn he rises in the dark,
navigates past den and kitchen

to the table and straight-backed chair.
Get down to work! God hath placed the living coal
upon thy tongue. Prophesy
the wolf gliding past the door,
eyes cold as Homer's,
trout stacked in spawning colors,
the rank and file of wanderlust.

He slides his hand across the table's grain
the way a blind man reads a face
he counts on staying. The way a batter
fearing the end of his streak
touches the hunchback's hump. He prays
words come to fill the room with angels
hailing him blessed of all carpenters,
all fathers getting it down
for sons to read.

Breakdown

He forgot her in Waxahachie, the Exxon station.
The trooper who pulled him over outside of Dallas
reported he looked surprised. The wife
had asked for the key to the rest room
and turned in time to see him drive away.
The attendant found a twenty
weighted on top of the Unleaded.

He apologized of course, then folded down
the back seat and lay on his side,
arms and knees tucked to his chest,
head pillowed on the rolled-up sleeping bag
the last boy forgot, packing for college.
The wife explained he was lost
without the children.
She set the cruise control for home.

He woke only once,
the flatlands outside of Weatherford,
and saw, or dreamed he saw,
two hawks clinched in free-fall coupling.
He shut his eyes as his father had done
that afternoon they watched a tightrope artist slip
across the wire between two downtown buildings.
Sometimes hawks forgot the earth was coming up.

Welcome Home, Stranger

You knew one day you'd find yourself alone,
Sunday, 6:00 a.m., an hour when no one
under forty is awake and hungry,
combing back streets for the one diner
that must be open.

You home in
on the buzzing neon sign
that almost spells CAFE,
the scent of coffee
acrid as napalm.

You know what to expect:
the drunk in khaki work pants
reading his fortune
in stains on the counter.

The woman everybody knows
in her orange formica booth,
curling her mouth around a word
thick as phlegm, a laugh floating up
from the bottom of a lake.

The night watchman tapping his ashes
in the amber dish. He nods to you
then drags on the cigarette,
cocks his head toward the ceiling,
its corrugated tin stars,
and fires a perfect 0.

Even the waitress is someone
you've expected—the grey synthetic sweater,

the bruise her makeup couldn't cover.
She fades between the tables rationing coffee,
reminding the watchman of his bladder.

She thinks her smile your only hope,
her asking, "What'll you have?"
an invitation you must accept.

Paul Completes the Path to Sainthood

All things work together for good
to them that love God.
I, Paul, a willing prisoner of Jehovah,
bound over to the centurion Julius
for passage across the sea to Rome,
declare the irony of any port called Fair Havens,
of any favorable breeze that springs up
sudden as anger, as the voice of God
above an ordinary road.
Take no comfort in barns brimming over,
in anything complacent as an empire,
precarious as a sailing vessel.

I warned Julius not to test the sea—
nature's metaphor for change,
but what Roman ever listens
before his only other option is the fish's belly?
On the fourteenth night of being driven
willy-nilly across the Adriatic,
of being hungry enough to believe a Jew,
Julius and his men clung to my words like planks
floating toward drowning sailors.
I promised not a hair of their heads would be lost,
God would return the sun and stars.

When we struck the shoal,
those who could swim made for shore.
The others grabbed for wreckage that would hold them up.
All 276 of us arrived at Malta,
island of hospitable natives

who pulled us from the sea and built a fire.
A viper drawn to the heat
attached itself to my hand.
The natives expected me to swell and die—
a criminal reaping divine justice.
So when I shook the creature into the fire
indifferent as a man slapping a mosquito,
they said I was a god.
I did what I could— laying my hands
on the chief's father, healing his fever,
and other persons on the island.

Come spring, we set sail
in a ship whose figurehead was the Twins,
my birth sign— Saul:Paul; Damascus:Rome—
proof God delights in irony.
I knew it hurt Julius's feelings
when he asked what I had to laugh about
and I said, "A private joke."
He had grown to love me,
so I put my arm around his shoulders
like a father comforting his child,
and asked had I ever told him about the time
God burst upon my sight?

St. Francis of Abilene

My friend has strained his back
lifting the lens of his telescope in place.
I teased him whether anything good came out of Cleveland
by parcel post in a brown truck predictable as a sermon.
He laughed and said God moves in mysterious vehicles.
I know my friend is on the lookout for Jehovah.
Pretending to count Saturn's rings,
he studies the face of Mars.

I love him for his lies, more perfectible
than mine jostled down the wide but crowded path.
He can't straighten up, but won't concern a doctor
over so small a hurt he knows will right itself in time
which he improves by watching.

For now, his eyes are focused on his office floor.
In the midst of my harangue—compressed vertebrae,
ruptured discs—he bends closer to the linoleum,
mosaic of the Milky Way, having spied a bug
with folded wings, antennae tracking my friend's belief
that all such should be rescued on a piece of paper,
lifted to the window he cannot raise,
and asks, with no embarrassment, for my help—
a sinner, who without his counsel would have squashed it.

The Writer-In-Residence Interrupts
My Scheduled Run

He swears I'm not happy unless exhausted,
gaunt as Gandhi. He's certain I'm one of those Jews
born too late for Hitler's chambers,
compensating, as Freud would say,
by jogging in nylon shorts and baseball cap
in the high noon oven of West Texas streets,
dodging pickups and ridicule. I laugh, confess
I'm not Jewish and take no pleasure in running.
He scratches his head and says, "You think
you'll live forever." On *earth* he means.
Maybe I did when I could click ten miles
between the twelve o'clock whistle and 1:15,
but now I'm down to three and a long shower,
not even the excuse of Vietnam—extraneous shrapnel
inching up the veins. And the bone
shaved from my lower back, too common for complaint.
"So maybe you wish to die like Housman's athlete?"
Too late again. I'm forty-seven, a ridiculous age
for baring the body in public.
Any kid on the playground runs faster.
He's bound to figure this out, but I can't wait.
The least pause and muscles start to cool.
I ease off down the street, let him have his say:
"It's guilt! You mark my word."

Just Off Beulah Street

He hung out at the bus station for a week,
frequented used car lots North 1st and Oak.
An old man in animal skins whispered
where to find the Hubcap King.

A plywood shed on cinder blocks
set back between a welder's shop
and the auto wrecking yard
overgrown with Johnson Grass and goats.

A sign: the ragged lid
of a cardboard box hand-lettered
in crayon by some child—HONK FOR ROY—
with ROY toppled down the side.

He had expected someone big,
in overalls, no shirt,
arms bulging like baby moons, teeth
dripping tobacco, the last pilgrim's fingers.

Roy turned out thin and blond, bald in front,
wire-rimmed glasses curled around each ear.
He wore a sky-blue shirt,
an Army Surplus flight jacket.

A padlock on the shed.
Only Roy knew the combination,
preceding him through the door
like a priest parting the veil.

A blinding light,
his eyes trying to focus: chrome

wall to wall, not a smudge or dent in sight.
Everywhere a convex mirror reflecting him

falling to his knees,
fumbling with the laces of his shoes.

Laying On of Hands

Only with dogs and children
and sometimes a woman weeping
on a bus station bench, hands
folded across her face like a veil.

The stranger passing
can only bring himself to stand
beside her, allow his hand
to settle on her shoulder, fingertips
touching, then lifting, then lighting
poised, muscles taut
for flight at the first ripple.

Only in a public place:
soldiers too sober to notice
a plain woman on a bench.
Widows on pensions, touring America,
passes clutched deep in pants' pockets.
College kids lost in travel diaries.

Only the janitor, himself invisible as khaki,
sees as he kneels beside the bench
to save his back retrieving
the paper coffee cup—its handles
the halves of a valentine,
unfolding wings,

a woman rising
in a man's overcoat, wiping her eyes
with a wadded hankie and laughing
at nothing . . . nothing at all.

To My Sons on Father's Day

You would have liked me
younger, careless,
my hair wild
like I'd just swung off a Harley.
I didn't talk much then,
thought nothing interesting but the weekend.
Everyone died at thirty.

Could you believe
I had this rolled and pleated Ford
and a girl from Waxahachie?
How about turning twenty-one on the coast
walking the Santa Monica waves,
dancing the Monkey with a topless waitress?

I understand.
You've only known me after Nam,
marriage vows
I raised my hand
and swore to honor.

What happened was
I didn't die
and learned to read headlines.

Thank you for the tie
and after-shave lotion.
The tee shirt with the cartoon penguin,
top hat apologetic in his hand.

Notes

The Biblical passages draw upon the language of the
   Pauline epistles used in *The American Standard
   Version* (1901) and in *The King James Version.*

The scenes depicted in the poems with the apostle Paul as
   persona are based on selected events from the life of
   Paul as outlined in the book of *Acts.* My immediate
   source was *The New Jerusalem Bible.*

The Tongues of Men and of Angels is the 1995 selection in the TTUP Invited Poetry Series. The publication of this book was generously supported by the Hardin-Simmons University Academic Foundation.